Severn Valley
Recollections

Contents

First published in 2010
ISBN 978 1 85794 353 5

Silver Link Publishing Ltd
The Trundle
Ringstead Road
Great Addington
Kettering
Northants NN14 4BW

Tel/Fax: 01536 330588
email: sales@nostalgiacollection.com
Website: www.nostalgiacollection.com
British Library Cataloguing in Publication Data
A catalogue record for this book is available from the
British Library.
Printed and bound in Czech Republic

Acknowledgments

As with any book project, there are
mumerous personalities and institutions
that help bring the idea to fruition. This
may be a small book but large thanks are
due to, especially, the photographers who
allowed their precious work to be used, to
Joan Kimberley, to Peter Townsend who
has given of his equally precious time as
well as his design skills; and to the Severn
Valley Railway who have been unstinting in
their support and co-operation in enabling
your author and contributors to capture
the images. This volume is by way of a
tribute to all of them.

Title page: **BEWDLEY** The view of the
station from the southern approach, on 13
June 2009, looking for all the world as it might
have done in the latter years of BR operation
prior to closure. *John Stretton*

Left: **BRIDGNORTH** The end of the line!
On 24 September 2005, 'Hall' 4-6-0 No 7903
Foremarke Hall has completed its journey from
Kidderminster and prepares to uncouple and
run round its train. *John Stretton*

Introduction by Peter Townsend

As I write this in January 2010 it doesn't seem possible to me, who was born halfway through the 20th Century, that we are entering the eleventh year of the 21st Century!

I lived in Swindon from the age of seven, for a number of years and an interest in railways was, one could say, inevitable. Not, I hasten to add, because of being in the queue for the Wednesday afternoon tour of the works when I should have been at school! Not even because the careers teacher at the initial interview would invariably ask each boy if he was 'going insde', which meant the railway workshops, not prison, to a Swindon boy. It was inevitable simply because in those far off days

'EVERY BOY WANTED TO BE A TRAIN DRIVER'!

(Well almost!).
Back then we woke up to ice on the windows in winter inside and out, pea soupers (thick fog or smog) were common, *The Clean Air Act* had still to take effect and smoke billowed from numerous chimneys the length and breadth of the country. The mills, foundries, quarries and mines were a hive of activity and there was an industry matched to a town - Kidderminster made carpets, Witney made Blankets, Sheffield made cutlery and all things steel, Birmingham made jewellry, motor-bikes, small arms and of course chocolate! Coventry made cars, Glasgow built ships as did Barrow, Gateshead and Belfast and so on and so on. We as kids just knew these things - the country seemed to be far more of a major player in world manufacturing.

Today we live in a fast moving, high powered, digitized, internet, email world. A world in which such topics as 'global markets', 'bankers' bonuses', 'MPs' expenses', 'scrappage schemes for cars and certain boilers' and 'global warming' make headlines. We are told that we live in a 'service economy' - do we take this to mean *'we can no longer, want or need to manufacture or build major things'* - I for one certainly hope we don't!

So, you might ask what has all that got to do with The Severn Valley Railway and this book in particular?

Well to explain...

Visiting the Severn Valley Railway means different things to different people and that is probably why it is so popular.

The locomotives and rolling stock of course are centre stage - but this railway is so much more if one looks in to the detail! There are so many more aspects to the railway - old advertising signs of long lost products bringing back memories for some while mystifying perhaps the inquisitive young who have never heard of them. The signalling, the point rodding, the lamps, the fire buckets, the urinal on platform 3 at Bewdley proudly embossed with the Glasgow Foundaries name that made it. The names of manufacturers can be found on items all over the railway - names that were in many cases from a different age, names of once proud companies many of which have passed into history. There is a pride that lives on here - just a glance at the smartly turned out hard working staff, the majority of whom are volunteers, will confirm this.

So, is this just a case of looking back with rose tinted spectacles to a time when it was 'all so much better then' a hankering to bring back the old days?
Well NO not really. For me this railway and others like it are both important and valuable. They are important because they are living reminders of our heritage, they are informative and educational - they not only bring history and nostalgia to life but through the excellent volunteer schemes they enable young and old to take part, to mix with each other, to learn and to preserve our heritage. They also demonstrate skills, ways and methods of working that need to be maintained and nurtured for the generations that will follow all of us.

These railways are valuable also because they provide us with a place to relax, unwind and enjoy life. If you doubt me, I invite you, preferably on a warm summers day, to buy a ticket to one of the tranquil wayside stations along the route, then to sit on one of the many benches, and simply watch the day go by!

But first please relax and enjoy these pictorial recollections with author John Stretton...

CELEBRATIONS!

Right: Over the years, the Severn Valley Railway has enjoyed various celebrations and received many plaudits, accolades and awards. Not least was the one received in 2008 in recognition of the railway's recovery from the disastrous floods of the previous year. Pride and pleasure come together as a plaque is received, recording the railway's success in...

"THE NATIONAL RAILWAY HERITAGE AWARDS 2008" when the railway was awarded the **Ian Allan Publishing HERITAGE RAILWAY OF THE YEAR AWARD"**. David Allan chairman of *Ian Allan Publishing Ltd (centre)* presented the award to The Severn Valley Railway represented here by Nick Ralls (SVR General Manager) and David Williams (Chairman). *Peter Townsend*

Left: One of the more recent celebrations was that commemorating the end of steam in 1968. 40 years later, to the day, the famous '1T57' last train was 'recreated' with 'Black 5' 4-6-0 No 45110 making a non-stop run from Kidderminster to Bridgnorth on 11 August 2008. Immediately prior to departure, David Porter (right) – the saviour of the locomotive all those years ago – discusses one or two stories of that deliverance from the cutter's torch with Ron Lawson, winner of a competition sponsored by *WH Smith, Silver Link* and *Steam Railway Magazine* to drive the locomotive from Kidderminster to Bridgnorth and return. *Peter Rowlands*

BRIDGNORTH

BRIDGNORTH A Typical scene at this northern terminus on 21 September 2008 2-6-2T No 4566 stands with doors open anticipating more travellers, before running south to Kidderminster. *John Stretton*

BRIDGNORTH Diesels are not ignored by the SVR! Providing visual variety resting in the shed yard, is 'Class 25' No D7633 in the early BR two-tone green livery. *Peter Townsend*

Right: **BRIDGNORTH** In BR steam days, engines often spent time on shed after their journey, for coal, water and any other attention that might be needed. On 7 September 1978, 'Britannia' 4-6-2 No. 70000 *Britannia* does just that, backing into the shed yard after bringing its train from Bewdley. Note the loco's spotless condition and the white cab roof adornment at this time. *James Besley, John Stretton collection*

Below: **BRIDGNORTH** Over the years, there have been many 'guest' locomotives visiting the SVR, old and new. One of the former, certainly in design - note for

example the very open cab - is 'Dukedog' No 9017, proudly wearing its *Earl of Berkeley* nameplates above the outside frames, seen resting on shed between duties on 11 August 2008. New from Swindon Works in 1938, it is more usually seen on the Bluebell Railway. *Peter Rowlands*

Opposite: **BRIDGNORTH** Further inside the shed, on 13 August 1980, is the 1935 pioneer 'Black 5', owned by the National Railway Museum and here in the guise of LMS No.5000. The workshops at Bridgnorth have earned justifiable respect and admiration through the years, for their part in repairing or restoring locomotives. *Robin Leleux*

Above: **BRIDGNORTH** A recent recipient of the SVR's 'tender loving care' is 'Flying Pig' 2-6-0 No 43106. Captured in the sunshine of 15 June 2009, in a brief spell from within the workshops, the loco is virtually complete and is only weeks from again re-entering service. Sadly, it was to suffer ignominy shortly after that return, with its tender derailing and damaging track close to Hampton Loade station! *John Stretton*

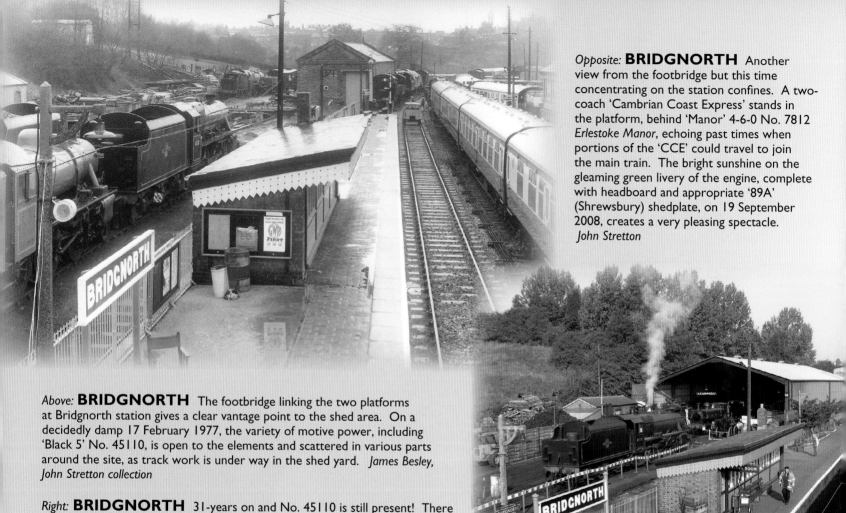

Opposite: **BRIDGNORTH** Another view from the footbridge but this time concentrating on the station confines. A two-coach 'Cambrian Coast Express' stands in the platform, behind 'Manor' 4-6-0 No. 7812 *Erlestoke Manor*, echoing past times when portions of the 'CCE' could travel to join the main train. The bright sunshine on the gleaming green livery of the engine, complete with headboard and appropriate '89A' (Shrewsbury) shedplate, on 19 September 2008, creates a very pleasing spectacle. *John Stretton*

Above: **BRIDGNORTH** The footbridge linking the two platforms at Bridgnorth station gives a clear vantage point to the shed area. On a decidedly damp 17 February 1977, the variety of motive power, including 'Black 5' No. 45110, is open to the elements and scattered in various parts around the site, as track work is under way in the shed yard. *James Besley, John Stretton collection*

Right: **BRIDGNORTH** 31-years on and No. 45110 is still present! There are changes, however, by 21 September 2008, with a shed building now in place to give shelter to both locos and staff, a coal supply has been installed on the far side of the yard and the background trees have grown. *Peter Rowlands*

Below: **BRIDGNORTH** The same vantage point but a different loco and, to the right, a different 'express'. We have already seen 'Dukedog' No. 9017 on shed here, but, on 21 September 2008, it is now gainfully employed and runs round its train before departing once more for Kidderminster. Note the carriage boards announcing the train as the Paddington-Milford Haven 'Boat Express'... but not to take passengers to the Irish Sea Ferry on this occasion! *John Stretton*

Below: **BRIDGNORTH** Steam engines are thirsty creatures and the smaller they are the less they can carry and, not infrequently, the more often they have to stop for refills. At the north end of Bridgnorth station, on 15 June 2009, the crew of ex-GWR 0-6-0PT No 7714 ensure that their charge is well equipped to continue its upcoming duties. At the end of this summer season, the loco was withdrawn from active service and was placed within The Engine House Museum at Highley. *John Stretton*

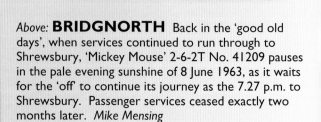

Above: **BRIDGNORTH** Back in the 'good old days', when services continued to run through to Shrewsbury, 'Mickey Mouse' 2-6-2T No. 41209 pauses in the pale evening sunshine of 8 June 1963, as it waits for the 'off' to continue its journey as the 7.27 p.m. to Shrewsbury. Passenger services ceased exactly two months later. *Mike Mensing*

Left: **BRIDGNORTH** Vital to the safe running of trains is the signalman. Whilst in the 21st century the remaining practitioners of the 'black arts' of signalling and the control of trains are usually situated many miles from the areas they control, former times saw signalboxes very close to the signals, points, gates, level crossings, etc that they supervised. These boxes are fondly remembered by many, with their magical array of instruments and large hand-operated levers. On 18 June 1983, Bridgnorth signalman Mike Thompson prepares to pull one of those levers in the course of his duty. *Bryan Hicks*

Below: **BRIDGNORTH** As well as passenger services, freight was a common feature on our railways and one which the signalman needed to pay especial attention, particularly if it had been delayed, or was stopping en-route to off load and/or pick up. An example of the latter stands at the southern end of the station, with 2-6-2T No. 4114 taking water as the guard finishes the tally of the train's consist in his 'little black book'. Note the distinctly varied rake of wagons! *Mike Mensing*

Right: **BRIDGNORTH** Our train awaits. Moments before departure, a visitor engages the driver in conversation, as 0-6-0PT No. 7714 quietly rests before given its head to run south to Highley on 19 September 2008. *John Stretton*

Left: **BRIDGNORTH** As we leave the station a glance back shows the extent of the shed and yard, adjacent to the station, as well as, to the right, the platform lengthened by the SVR to accommodate longer trains than would ever have been seen in BR days. *Peter Rowlands*

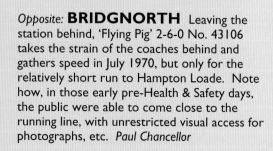

Opposite: **BRIDGNORTH** Leaving the station behind, 'Flying Pig' 2-6-0 No. 43106 takes the strain of the coaches behind and gathers speed in July 1970, but only for the relatively short run to Hampton Loade. Note how, in those early pre-Health & Safety days, the public were able to come close to the running line, with unrestricted visual access for photographs, etc. *Paul Chancellor*

Above right: **OLDBURY VIADUCT** Having left Bridgnorth and crossed the road bridges to the south of the station, 'Black 5' 4-6-0 No 45110 – here bearing its *RAF Biggin Hill* nameplates – accelerates near to the viaduct on 12 September 1971, on its way to Knowlesands Tunnel with another train terminating at Hampton Loade. *Bryan Hicks*

Below right: **HAMPTON LOADE** Until 1974 this station, some 4½ miles from Bridgnorth, was the southern extremity of the burgeoning SVR. Not an easy place to reach by road, the new line's obvious popularity can be judged by the number of vehicles finding space in the very limited parking area. In the station on 25 May 1970, '2251 Class' 0-6-0 No. 3205, one of the early locos handling the services, has run round its train and prepares to make the return journey to Bridgnorth. *Ben Ashworth*

HAMPTON LOADE

Below: HAMPTON LOADE
Going back to pre-restoration days, we look north to witness 0-6-0PT No. 8718 entering the station with a short 'up' freight. With another mixed rake of wagons in tow, the fireman looks ahead, token in hand, ready for exchange with the signalman and permission to continue the journey south on 16 April 1954. *John Edgington*

Far left: **HAMPTON LOADE** We again look north but this time 21 years later. On 26 August 1975, the location is no longer a terminus, with the extension to Bewdley opening in the previous year and the passing loop within the station confines now put to good use to enhance the passenger services. 'Jinty' 0-6-0 No. 47383 approaches from Bridgnorth, with tokens again about to be exchanged, which will then allow 2-6-2T No. 4566, in this platform, to continue its travels north. *Bryan Hicks*

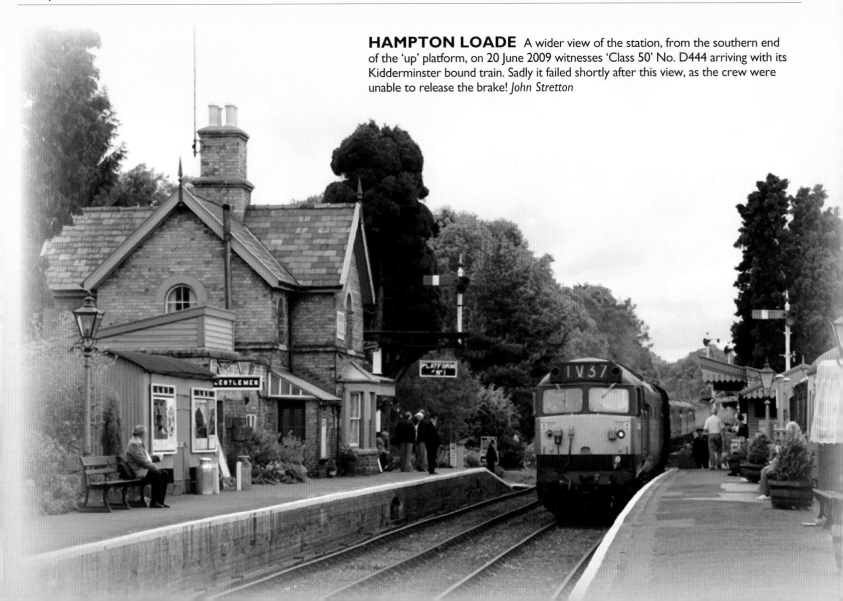

HAMPTON LOADE A wider view of the station, from the southern end of the 'up' platform, on 20 June 2009 witnesses 'Class 50' No. D444 arriving with its Kidderminster bound train. Sadly it failed shortly after this view, as the crew were unable to release the brake! *John Stretton*

HAMPTON LOADE The value of the loop here is shown on 20 June 2009. The failed train on the previous page is still in the platform, but operations have not totally ground to a halt as 2-6-0 No. 46443 arrives with its rake of carriages bound for Bridgnorth. *John Stretton*

SEVERN VALLEY RAILWAY
Special ticket issued to mark five years
of the Severn Valley Railway as a volun-
tary organisation and the REOPENING
OF THE RAILWAY 23rd MAY 1970
BRIDGNORTH
EARDINGTON
HAMPTON LOADE
AND RETURN
FIRST CLASS   FARE 9/-
0001

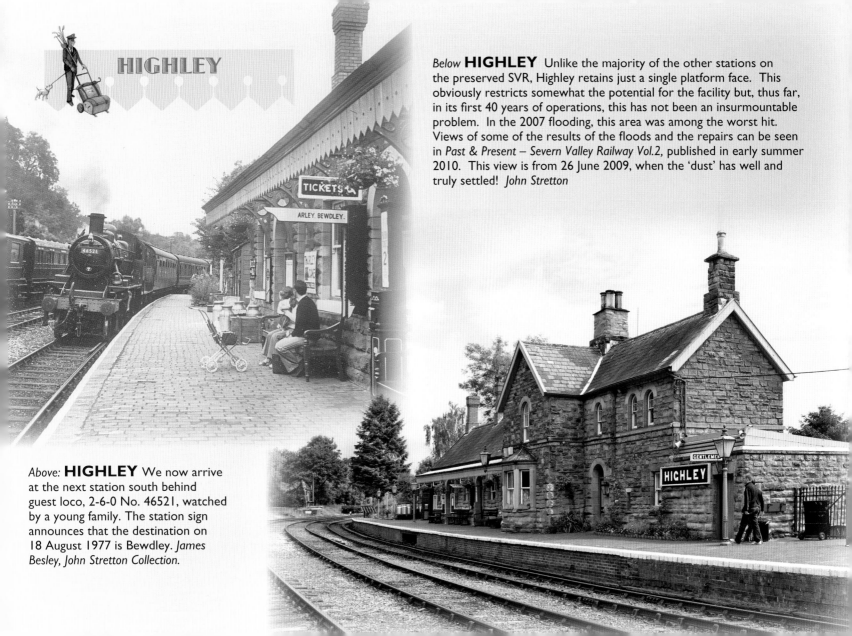

HIGHLEY

Below **HIGHLEY** Unlike the majority of the other stations on the preserved SVR, Highley retains just a single platform face. This obviously restricts somewhat the potential for the facility but, thus far, in its first 40 years of operations, this has not been an insurmountable problem. In the 2007 flooding, this area was among the worst hit. Views of some of the results of the floods and the repairs can be seen in *Past & Present – Severn Valley Railway Vol.2,* published in early summer 2010. This view is from 26 June 2009, when the 'dust' has well and truly settled! *John Stretton*

Above: **HIGHLEY** We now arrive at the next station south behind guest loco, 2-6-0 No. 46521, watched by a young family. The station sign announces that the destination on 18 August 1977 is Bewdley. *James Besley, John Stretton Collection.*

Below: **HIGHLEY** Whilst a majority of visitors to preserved railways prefer to see steam, diesels do have their place and their followers, with ex-BR 'Class 50s' especially popular. With The Engine House, hiding among the trees in the background, No. D444 approaches with the 0950 Kidderminster-Bridgnorth service of 20 June 2009. If you look closely, very closely you can just see the 'second man' crouched in the loco's doorway ready to exchange tokens on entering the station. *John Stretton*

Above: HIGHLEY Into the 21st century, the station has been augmented by The Engine House Museum, newly constructed close by, on the site of the old coal sidings. This view from 20 June 2009 shows the attractively styled building, which houses many locomotives and other artefacts that add real value to a visit to this part of the railway. *John Stretton*

THE ENGINE HOUSE

W.D. No 600 *Gordon* is seen in service on *page 33,* but into the 21st Century is safely entombed in the museum (*above*), seen on 6 November 2009. The same day also displayed a loco footplate including 'life' in the firebox! The enamel 'Billie-can' and mug were the 'must have' items for the steam age footplate crew - a tradition carried on by many of the drivers and firemen of preserved lines today! *Both John Stretton*

ARLEY

PASSENGERS ARE NOT ALLOWED TO CROSS THE RAILWAY EXCEPT BY THE BRIDGE

Gt. Western Ry.   Gt. Western Ry.
OLDBURY   OLDBURY
& LANGLEY GN   & LANGLEY GN
TO
ARLEY G.W
via Cradley & Bewdley
THIRD CLASS
3/4 G Fare 3/4 C
ARLEY G.W   ARLEY G.W
FOR CONDITI   SEE BACK (W.)
178   178

Opposite page: **NR. HIGHLEY**
Continuing our journey southwards, we are passed by a northbound freight on 11 September 1982. Dressed in its one-time BR(W) all-green livery, 2-6-0 No. 46521 has a mixed rake of wooden-bodied wagons that appear to be carrying waste from engineering work. Note the proximity of the River Severn beyond the train. *Bryan Hicks*

Right: **ARLEY** The station has long been a popular stopping off point on the railway, even in its pre-restoration days, due to the attractive surrounding countryside and the walk down to the river. A slightly unusual vantage point is taken on 26 August 1975, to witness 2-6-2T No. 4566 enter with its train from Bridgnorth to Bewdley. The fireman hangs out to exchange his token with what must be one of the youngest station 'staff' ever to operate this procedure! Where is the young lad now, one wonders! *Bryan Hicks*

ARLEY Whilst passenger locomotives are designed to run boiler first, there are times when this is not possible. On 26 September 2009, 'Hall' No. 4936 *Kinlet Hall* draws to a halt with its service to Bridgnorth. *John Stretton*

Background below: **ARLEY** In cold weather the locomotive footplate can be a welcoming place but, in the heat of summer, there is no room to escape the intense heat of the fire in the boiler! In the station on 13 June 2009, the crew of 'Manor' No. 7812 *Erlestoke Manor* will no doubt be sweating off a few pounds as they operate the 1445 Bridgnorth-Kidderminster passenger service. *John Stretton*

Right: **ARLEY** The view from the road bridge that crosses the railway at the southern end of the station platform sees 'Manor' No. 7802 *Bradley Manor* arriving on 13 June 2009, with the 1450 Kidderminster-Bridgnorth train. Seen just moments before the arrival of 7812 above, this gave a rare opportunity of seeing two 'Manors' in Arley at the same time. *John Stretton*

Below: **VICTORIA BRIDGE** Most views of the bridge illustrate the wide span, but here we are now on the bridge, with a celebrity.

On 28 September 1985 the ancient structure takes the weight of 'Castle' No. 7029 *Clun Castle* and its train in full flight, on their way north to Arley and Bridgnorth. One of just eight preserved of 166 'Castles' built, *Clun* did not appear from Swindon Works until 1950, two years into British Railways following Nationalisation but still constructed to the GWR design. Usually based at Tyseley, in the Birmingham Railway Museum, it was here providing a real treat for the SVR and its visitors. *Bryan Hicks*

Below: **VICTORIA BRIDGE** When built in 1861, this bridge boasted the largest cast iron clear span in the World and it has been a cause célèbre for photographers ever since. However, this view shows the northern exit from it, with the river just glimpsed in the bottom right corner, as 'Manor' No. 7802 *Bradley Manor* leaves its vapour trail across the landscape, heading towards Arley in 2005. *Paul Chancellor*

Right: **EYEMORE** A little south of Victoria Bridge, the railway passes Eyemore Wood. On 22 May 1988, 2-6-2T No. 4566 is again seen out on the line, heading south with another Bridgnorth-Kidderminster working. New in 1924, from Swindon Works, this loco has been a stalwart on the SVR ever since its withdrawal from BR in April 1962 and rescue from Dai Woodham's Barry Docks scrapyard eight years later. *Bryan Hicks*

TRIMPLEY RESERVOIR Continuing the GWR tradition from steam into diesel days, the Western Region of BR went its own way, authorising the construction of diesel-hydraulic locos as opposed the diesel-electric format favoured elsewhere! Though not long-lived, the 'Westerns' were much loved by enthusiasts at the end, not least for their design, characteristics and colour schemes. One of those latter variants is seen on No. D1062 *Western Courier* as it climbs to pass the reservoir on 20 October 1979, on its way north from Bewdley. *Bryan Hicks*

Above: **NORTHWOOD HALT** Stuck in the middle of nowhere, this Halt could easily be overlooked and/or neglected by the railway but, happily, this is not so, as proved by the SVR being awarded

THE G.N.E.R. VOLUNTEERS AWARD FOR 2007

by the NATIONAL RAILWAY HERITAGE AWARDS

A celebratory party are here seen inspecting the site in appropriately, the Inspection Saloon. *Peter Townsend*

Below left: **NORTHWOOD** Less than a mile north of Bewdley, the twin tracks parted company, as the branch to Tenbury Wells swung westwards. This latter alignment is to the left in this view, on a slightly falling gradient in contrast to the 'main line'. In 1959, 'Standard 3' 2-6-2T No. 82004 is under no strain as it moves its three coach load towards Bewdley with another service from Shrewsbury. *Mike Mensing*

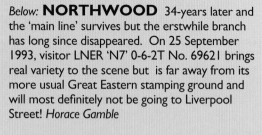

BEWDLEY

Below: **NORTHWOOD** 34-years later and the 'main line' survives but the erstwhile branch has long since disappeared. On 25 September 1993, visitor LNER 'N7' 0-6-2T No. 69621 brings real variety to the scene but is far away from its more usual Great Eastern stamping ground and will most definitely not be going to Liverpool Street! *Horace Gamble*

Right: **BEWDLEY** We have now arrived at the major intermediate station on the current SVR. Once a junction both north and south of the station, it is now a straight run through to and from Kidderminster and Bridgnorth. On 24 September 2005, 0-6-0PT No. 1501 pulls into the platform with the lunchtime departure from Bridgnorth, bound for the terminus at Kidderminster. *John Stretton*

Top right: **BEWDLEY** A move onto the footbridge between platforms brings this view of one of BR's attempts to stem increasing running costs on the branch. GWR Railcar No. W22W arrives on 15 August 1959, as a three-car WR Suburban DMU set moves out of the station, in the distance, with the 2 p.m. service out of Birmingham (Snow Hill). The view to the housing on the right in the 21st century makes for an interesting comparison. *Mike Mensing*

Bottom right: **BEWDLEY** Turning round to look south, No. W20W arrives with a local service on a very damp looking 26 April 1958. Two ladies wait to board and the porter has a healthy load of parcels to put on board, while the other member of the station staff looks as though he is about to pole vault over these parcels! All credit to the current SVR that incredibly little has changed over the years at this location. *R J Buckley, Initial Photographics collection*

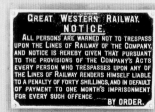

GREAT WESTERN RAILWAY.
NOTICE.
ALL PERSONS ARE WARNED NOT TO TRESPASS UPON THE LINES OF RAILWAY OF THE COMPANY, AND NOTICE IS HEREBY GIVEN THAT PURSUANT TO THE PROVISIONS OF THE COMPANY'S ACTS EVERY PERSON WHO TRESPASSES UPON ANY OF THE LINES OF RAILWAY RENDERS HIMSELF LIABLE TO A PENALTY OF FORTY SHILLINGS, AND IN DEFAULT OF PAYMENT TO ONE MONTH'S IMPRISONMENT FOR EVERY SUCH OFFENCE.
BY ORDER.

Below: **BEWDLEY** In the period that the station was the southern terminus of the railway, trains would often depart from Platform 2. On 10 September 1978, old friend 2-6-2T No. 4566 waits while it has its water tanks replenished by hose pipe (!), before returning to Bridgnorth. *Bryan Hicks*

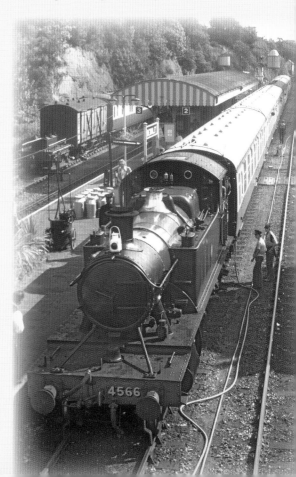

BEWDLEY The infrastructure is just as important as the trains in completing the visitor experience. Here, on 31 July 2007, the station has old style suitcases, hanging baskets and a clear timetable for the day to add to the attractive original brickwork. *Peter Townsend*

BEWDLEY Once loathed by enthusiasts when first introduced in large numbers in the 1950s, the 'first generation' Diesel Multiple Units (DMUs) later became viewed much more affectionately. The overall green livery, with yellow stripes, front whiskers, etc., are now looked upon with great nostalgia and November 1960 vintage Derby 'Class 108' DMBS No. M51935, seen here between duties on 21 February 2007, shows why. *Peter Townsend*

Above: **BEWDLEY** Another departure from Platform 2 is seen from the ground level four years earlier, on 22 June 1974, shortly after the extension to this new terminus. Ex-LMS 2-6-0 No 46443 is the centre of attention, gleaming proudly in the mid-summer sunshine. *Dennis Weaver, John Stretton collection*

Left: **BEWDLEY** The length that a railway will go to in attempting recreation of past events is gloriously encapsulated here, as one of the station staff struggles to shift a load of milk churns on 30 August 1983. *Bryan Hicks*

Below left: **BEWDLEY** This ex-WD 2-10-0 is certainly one of the largest locomotives to work on the SVR, if not the most powerful. Built in 1943 for the Ministry of Defence by North British and numbered 3651, it ended its working life at Longmoor Military Railway, as No. 600 *Gordon*. It is seen about to depart for Bridgnorth on 22 June 1974, in its bright blue coat. After helping the railway in its early years, the loco was withdrawn from service and is now a prime exhibit in The Engine House Museum. *Dennis Weaver, John Stretton collection*

Below right: **BEWDLEY** On occasion, not least in Galas, trains will run into Platform 3. One such, on 24 September 2005, is handled by 0-6-2T No 6619, attractively decked out in BR plain black with the original 'cycling lion' logo on the tank. The floral display, the tasteful station paintwork and the 'cliff side' all add to the portrait. *John Stretton*

Right: **BEWDLEY** Moving past the engine and turning round, the driver takes a moment to rest from his exertions and concentration! Although the carriage board announces 'Milford Haven' I doubt this train will be attempting that sort of journey on 24 September 2005! *John Stretton*

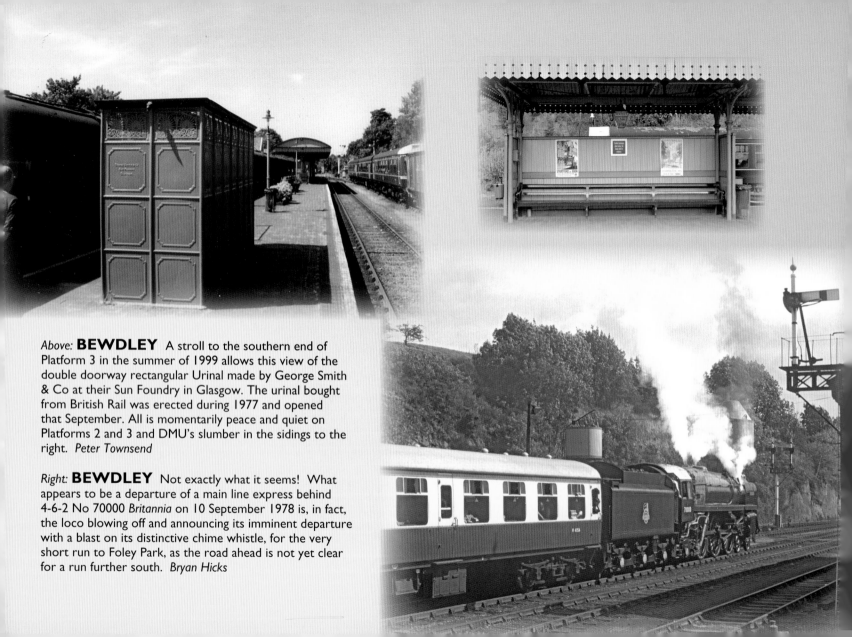

Above: **BEWDLEY** A stroll to the southern end of Platform 3 in the summer of 1999 allows this view of the double doorway rectangular Urinal made by George Smith & Co at their Sun Foundry in Glasgow. The urinal bought from British Rail was erected during 1977 and opened that September. All is momentarily peace and quiet on Platforms 2 and 3 and DMU's slumber in the sidings to the right. *Peter Townsend*

Right: **BEWDLEY** Not exactly what it seems! What appears to be a departure of a main line express behind 4-6-2 No 70000 *Britannia* on 10 September 1978 is, in fact, the loco blowing off and announcing its imminent departure with a blast on its distinctive chime whistle, for the very short run to Foley Park, as the road ahead is not yet clear for a run further south. *Bryan Hicks*

Above: **BEWDLEY** The south signalbox vitally controls southern access and departures. On 20 June 2009, 2-6-0 No. 46443 begins a light-engine run to Kidderminster. *John Stretton*

Right: **BEWDLEY** Time has moved on and arrivals now come from the 'deepest' south in Kidderminster! Another 'monster' engine steams into Bewdley, as 'Duchess' 4-6-2 No 6233 Duchess of Sutherland – once 'land-locked' within Bressingham Steam Museum in Norfolk – makes light of its load on 23 September 2006. With its magnificent 'Royal Scot' headboard, it presents the epitome of visual attraction for the visitor. *Horace Gamble*

Opposite: **BEWDLEY** Bewdley South (aka Sandbourne) Viaduct crosses the valley very soon after leaving the station. On Bank Holiday Monday, 1 August 1960, when the various lines radiating from Bewdley were all still in action, an unidentified GWR '5101 Class' 2-6-2T crosses with the 4.58 p.m. Tenbury Wells-Hartlebury train. Kidderminster was not the usual destination in those times. *David Johnson*

Above: **BEWDLEY** We now resume our journey south. Passing the South signalbox, with the phalanx of semaphore signals guarding against any conflicting movements, 'star turn' 4-4-0 No. 3440 *City of Truro* gathers speed on the run to Kidderminster on 28 September 1985. *Bryan Hicks*

BEWDLEY Travelling in the opposite direction, another visitor, ex-Port Talbot Railway 0-6-0ST No. 813, approaches the viaduct on 26 September 2009 in glorious late afternoon light, as the 1653 departure from Kidderminster. *John Stretton*

BEWDLEY Just yards further towards Kidderminster another elderly ex-LNER loco approaches the same spot. Some 45 minutes prior to No. 813, on 26 September 2009, ex-GNR 0-6-2T No. 1744 (ex-BR No. 69523) has an appropriate rake of teak coaches in tow, as the 1620 from the southern terminus. A lineside fire at this point had delayed it and the hi-vis-vested fire-fighting SVR workers can be seen on either side of the line. Hanging from the cab, scanning the way ahead, is impresario Pete Waterman. *John Stretton*

FOLEY PARK TUNNEL The route to Kidderminster tunnels through the landscape at Foley Park, making for entertainment for both passengers and engine crews! On Saturday, 25 September 1993, double-headed ex-GWR 2-6-2T No. 4566 and ex-LMS 0-6-0 No. 44422 emerge from the tunnel mouth, operating the 1325 Kidderminster-Bridgnorth service. *Horace Gamble*

KIDDERMINSTER

KIDDERMINSTER The BR engine shed was situated in the triangle of land between the main line from the town to Worcester and the branch line to Bewdley. Opened in 1932, replacing one that had previously been at the southern end of the main line station, it closed on 10 August 1964. In somewhat happier times, 2-6-0 No. 5394 stands in the yard on 7 April 1957, with the ramped coaling stage behind it. *J Davenport, Initial Photographics collection*

KIDDERMINSTER The comparative facility for the new SVR is closer to the town and is currently mostly open to the elements for the locos. On 12 June 2009, 'Class 50' No. 50135 (actually No 50035) Ark Royal stands in the yard, looking magnificent in its new, for both class and loco, 'Load Haul' livery. *John Stretton*

KIDDERMINSTER We approach our destination, but how many of today's visitors realise that the current SVR's terminus has been completely created from scratch by the railway, from the coal yard sidings that had once graced the site. On 12 June 2009, 'Manor' No. 7812 *Erlestoke Manor* leaves the SVR station with the 1210 service to Bridgnorth, while a DMU, right, leaves the main line station for Worcester. *John Stretton*

Below: **KIDDERMINSTER** After arrival, locomotives uncouple and run round their trains. On a VERY wet day, 2-6-0 No. 46443 prepares to move forward to complete the procedure. *Peter Townsend.*

Above: **KIDDERMINSTER** We have reached our final destination. Initially created with an open concourse, the travelling public are now protected from the elements. The elegant structure completes the vintage scene on 6 November 2009. *John Stretton*

LOCOMOTIVES

The final few images look at just a handful of the many and varied locomotives seen on the SVR over the past 40 years.

5051 Almost timeless, with only the more modern housing in the background evidencing that this is not from GWR days. On 30 September 1984, 'Castle' No. 5051 Earl Bathurst (but here wearing its former Drysllwyn Castle persona) prepares to back down into Kidderminster station, to form the 3.14 p.m. train to Bridgnorth, during its short one month stay on the railway. *Hugh Ballantyne*

5164 Resplendent in its immaculate GWR plain green livery, complete with 'GREAT WESTERN' on the tanks, 2-6-2T No. 5164 stands at Bewdley between duties on 26 September 2009. New from Swindon Works in 1930, it enjoyed a working life of 33 years before withdrawal on 6 April 1963, with homes including Tyseley, Newton Abbot and Pontypool Road sheds. *John Stretton*

Left: **6619** We have already seen No. 6619 resting at Bewdley on 24 September 2005, but here we have a closer view, giving a slightly better grasp of the bulk and power of this outwardly small loco. Swindon turned it out in 1928, for work in and around the coalfields of the South Wales valleys and it stayed there for most of its life. Barry shed was its home for many years and, following withdrawal in March 1963, it was but a short step to Dai Woodham's scrapyard on the nearby Docks in August 1964. Happily preservation beckoned, in the guise of the North Yorks Moors Railway. *John Stretton*

7812 When locos are seen in restored condition, it is often difficult to imagine a less glorious state. Seen at Bewdley in the summer of 1999, 'Manor' 4-6-0 No. 7812 *Erlestoke Manor* is not exactly in appalling condition but some of the work required to put it back into service can be imagined. *Peter Townsend*

7812 Here we are a little over 9 years later. On 21 September 2008, No. 7812 stands in Bridgnorth shed yard, gleaming in the sunshine, in company with 2-6-2T No. 5164. Emerging from Swindon Works at the time of the outbreak of WWII, 7812 was one of 30 built for passenger work on more secondary routes and spent much of its life in Devon/Cornwall and mid/west Wales. BR dispensed with it on 7 October 1965 and it travelled to Barry Docks the following June, from where it was saved for the SVR. *Peter Rowlands*

Above: **45110** The dramatic and near-fatal 'full story' of the salvation of 'Black 5' 4-6-0 No. 45110 is told in *BR STEAM – the Final Years 1965-68* (Silver Link Publishing), by saviour David Porter. Officially withdrawn early in September 1968, after being the final locomotive to work the infamous 'Ten Guinea Special' final rostered steam train '1T57' on BR the previous month, it has since spent most of its 'pampered' existence on the SVR. On 6 October 1984, it looks rather careworn, standing out of service alongside the shed wall at Bridgnorth. *Ray Ruffell, Silver Link Publishing collection*

Bottom left: **45110** Looking decidedly happier, the 'Black 5' is again in Bridgnorth shed yard, but this time in steam. However, the fire will soon be dropped and another spell of overhaul will begin as, on 11 August 2008, it has run the recreation of the '1T57' train and has run out of boiler ticket. Ever a popular loco on the SVR, many enthusiasts will be eager to see it back in service once again in the (hopefully not-too-distant) future. At the time of writing it is on static display at the National Railway Museum's Shildon site. *Peter Rowlands*

Above: **1054** The sole-surviving ex-LNWR 'Coal Tank' 0-6-2T is more normally at home on the Keighley & Worth Valley Railway but, on 21 September 1986, is enjoying an 'away break' at the SVR. It is here in 'original' condition, numbered as built at Crewe Works

in September 1888. It subsequently became LMS No. 7799 and then, following the creation of BR in 1948, No. 58926 in the subsequent numbering scheme. Finishing its working life in 1958, having latterly served at the upper and lower ends of the Heart of Wales line, it was bought privately. Both before and after Nationalisation it had an eventful life! *Bryan Hicks*

Above: **80079** By contrast, we finish the steam selection with the most modern of the locomotives in this section. 'Standard 4' No. 80079 emerged from Brighton Works in March 1954 and was immediately despatched to Plaistow shed, on the LT&S line to the east of London. Moving to the WR in 1962, it went to and stayed at Croes Newydd, from where the end came on 19 September 1965 – just 11½ years old! To Barry Docks in 1966, salvation came from the SVR in 1971. *Peter Townsend*

Left: **E6005** The BR 'Bo-Bo' Electro diesels (later 'Class 73') were introduced at the beginning of the 1960s as part of the 1955 Modernisation Plan. In poor external condition the 1962 vintage locomotive rests in Kidderminster shed yard on 12 June 2009, in company with No. 50135 *Ark Royal* and No. D444.

Inset: **ARK ROYAL** nameplate complete with crest as affixed to No. 50135.

Above: **12099**. One of 106 0-6-0 diesel-electric shunters introduced by the LMS in 1945, No. 12099 was new in 1952. Seen by Kidderminster turntable on 12 June 2009, the class became '11' in BR TOPS scheme of 1974.

Below left: **D3022** A derivative of the LMS type above, this class became '08' in TOPS reclassification. Also built in 1952 No. D3022 stands in the shed yard at Kiddeminster on the same day as No. 12099 above.

Below: **E6006** Also new in 1962 but in much more presentable external condition, ED No. E6006 stands in Bewdley station sidings, in company with one of the railways other Class 08s - No. D3937 *Gladys* - on 13 June 2009. *All John Stretton*

"Please do visit again soon!"

INDEX